HIGH SCHOOL MONOLOGUES
THEY HAVEN'T HEARD

Roger Karshner

Dramaline Publications
36-851 Palm View Road
Tancho Mirage, CA 92270
Phone 619/770-6076 Fax 619/770/4507

Cover art, John Sable

CONTENTS

YOUNG WOMEN

DORIS

Doris feels it's time for her parents to allow her to date without approval and supervision.

Every time I go out with new a guy I get, like, this big lecture from my parents. Like this big deal sit-down-and-discuss-every-detail-lecture, you know. The stuff they lay on me and put me through is really incredible. They want to know everything, and I mean—*everything*. Like every little thing about the guy. Like where he comes from. Like where do they think he comes from? Mars? Do they think I'm going out with, like, this total mutant, or something? I go out with guys from school, who else?

Then they want to know all about his parents. What they do, their background—you name it. Like I'm supposed to be this census taker, or something, and know all about his family, right? About how much money they make, how many johns they have in their house. . . . Jeez. I assume they're regular, okay people. Around here most parents are pretty neat. Neat but really square. Most of 'em are, like, out of an old sitcom, face it. The mothers are real mincy with tight little hair and the fathers are kind of gruff but understanding with corny senses of humor and cheap shoes. Kind of, like, right out of "Leave It To Beaver," you know. Then they want to meet the guy. How about that? This really makes a swell first impression on a guy, right? So, like, he has to come over before the date and meet my folks who stare at him and offer him cookies and ask him stupid questions, likewhat he wants to be when he grows up. (*A beat for response.*) No, I swear. Honest. They asked Bobby Grimes what he wanted to be, and when he told them a taxidermist, I thought my dad was going to vomit. It really turned me off, I know that. I mean, the thought of some guy touching you who has just stuffed a rabbit. Yuck!

It's a wonder I ever have a date. I mean, with all the stupid stuff I have to go through before I can go out with a guy; with my parents being, like, the CIA, the KGB, and Dick Tracy. You're lucky, Diane, you've got it made. You're parents are cool. Although, come to think of it, the next time you have a date maybe you should bring him on over and let my mom and dad check him out first. You go out with some real turkeys.

Never work with animals or children.

Anonymous. Show business maxim.

ALLISON

The deteriorating state of the environment is of great concern.

Over the weekend we went up to the Lake. We have a cabin up there. It's a neat place. Like with all this wilderness and wildlife all around. There are trees up there that are nearly two hundred years old. It's a very beautiful, peaceful place. At night you lie in bed and all you hear are the sounds of nature.

We've been going up there since I was a little kid. All of us. The whole family. But it's not the same. Things are changing. Like the lake, for instance. A few years ago you could see its bottom from anywhere, even the deepest spot. But not anymore. Not since a factory started dumping waste into the stream that feeds it. You should see how it looks now. It's become polluted and stagnant and murky. I not about to go swimming in it anymore. None of us will. We're afraid it's not safe.

I must have counted two-dozen dead fish up there this weekend. Floating on top of the water. The pollution is killing them off, upsetting the balance of nature, messing up the whole place. My father, and some of the other people, have complained to the company but so far nothing's been done.

If you know anything at all about nature, you realize how delicate it is and how easily it's upset by the encroachment of people and industry and how important it is for us to give it our respect. But we don't. It seems, like, we just don't give a damn.

We just keep on polluting and making excuses and making promises that we keep breaking over and over until something tragic happens. Like, that big mess up in Alaska. That could have been avoided if people had taken precautions.

I'm not for closing down businesses and putting people out of work or anything like that. Over reacting would be crazy. What I'm talking about here is us being more responsible, more sensible in dealing with these problems before they get way out of hand, that's all.

We're depleting the ozone layer, sucking up the forests, polluting the oceans and rivers and streams, screwing up our air, and blowing away the animals. Little by little we're trashing the planet. And the irony of the thing is, we may end up trashing is ourselves.

Just know your lines and don't bump into the furniture.
Noel Coward (1899–1973)

MOLLY

Molly tells of the courageousness of a fellow school mate whose heart, transplanted from an admirer, finally stopped functioning.

Cindy had her first heart transplant a little over three years ago. But the heart became diseased and she didn't have long to live, not unless she could find a proper donor. Her heart was donated by this guy, Jerry Castleman, who liked her a lot, who was really crazy about her. So, he told his parents that if anything ever happened to him that he wanted his heart to go to Cindy. Like, something was going to happen to Jerry Castleman, right? A guy in his condition. This super-healthy, buff guy who was into all kinds of sports, and everything.

But Jerry must have had, like, this feeling, this premonition, or something, you know. Because, just a few weeks later, he was killed in a freak motorcycle accident. So, they took his heart and transplanted it in Cindy and it saved her.

Cindy was in a couple of my classes. Math and science. She was a really neat, intelligent person who never complained or bitched even though she knew she was living on borrowed time. She had courage like you wouldn't believe. During the past three years, she had to go into the hospital twelve times, and it just had to be painful and scary for her every time. But when I'd ask her about it, she'd just smile and change the subject to something about me or somebody else. She was always concerned about others and their interests and problems and never talked about herself or her illness. She was really amazing.

Cindy died last week. She was my age—seventeen. She'd been waiting for another heart but they couldn't locate one in time. It was a sad thing. But, in a way, you know, it wasn't. Because all of us learned a lot from Cindy. We learned a lot about the real meaning of courage and strength and bravery. Cindy was a special person.

I always wanted to do what my mother did—get all dressed up, shoot people, fall in the mud. I never considered anything else.

Carrie Fisher (1956–)

SALLY

Sally expresses a mix of disdain and admiration for brilliant students.

Some kids have these brains so big they can't find hats to fit. They're, like, super-smart. But to me, they're big pains in the butt. Because most of them have this "Hey! look at me, I'm smarter than anyone" attitude and this smug smart-ass look on their faces. Maybe they've got this look because they're just plain smarter or maybe because they get off on being arrogant jerks. Who knows?

Susan Feinstein has a brain that could eat Cleveland, and an IQ long as a telephone number. She knows everything. More than the teacher, even. She comes up with stuff you wouldn't believe. Like,yesterday when Mrs. Hockhowser didn't know crap from Wheaties about what a jerboa was? Feinstein rattles off all this junk about it being a mouse-like rodent that lives in Asia and North Africa and looks like a kangaroo. Smart ass. If you ask me the mouse-like rodent is Feinstein.

But then, wait a minute, this isn't fair. Not really. Kids like Feinstein can't help it if they're born messed up and cut out to be know-it-alls. You can't blame them. If I were super-sharp, instead of a cork head, I'd probably be bored stiff sitting in a class with a bunch of retards, too.

Sometimes I watch Feinstein and she'll be looking out the window with this expression like she'd like to be anywhere else. And who can blame her? I mean, here she is, in this class she should be teaching, sitting around real bored with her intelligence going down the tubes.

High IQ kids should be graduated and put in college right away instead of having to put their brains on hold for four years. Holding back super-intelligent students is a waste.

I think Feinstein should be in college right now. And besides, it'd be a real relief getting a mouse-like rodent the hell out of my life.

> *Goodbye Norma Jean*
> *Though I never knew you at all*
> *You had the grace to hold yourself*
> *While those around you crawled.*
> *They crawled out of the woodwork*
> *And they whispered in your brain*
> *Set you on the treadmill*
> *And made you change your name.*
>
> Bernie Taupin. Lyrics from "Candle in the Wind".

JULIE

Julie believes adults are reactionary regarding sex.

There's a lot of controversy about sex-education and about teaching about AIDS in school; about how far they should go and how early they should start teaching it, and like that. As far as I'm concerned, they should start in educating kids about this stuff in kindergarten. But they won't because the parents will come unglued. So, the educators take it slow in order to avoid problems and confrontations. You'd think parents would want their kids to know the facts as early as possible.

I just read where less than ten percent of students up through the sixth grade are taught anything about AIDS. Less than ten percent! Can you believe it? Because people have got burger brains, that's why; because they've got these old-fashioned ideas; because they're still carrying around all these fears and superstitions about sex. Wow.

Here we have this life-threatening virus and we're reluctant to educate our children because, whoa, hey! Because we just can't talk about such a "terrible" subject as (*Spells it.*) S-E-X. Like sex is something new, right? Like kids don't ever think about it or have urges or questions or already don't know the score. Like teenagers don't know what's happening. Are they kidding? When are adults going to grow up and face facts and starting dealing in truth instead of behaving like a bunch of Medieval air heads?

In some states now they've got laws that make teachers stress not having sex till you get married. I wonder how many of the mental midgets who dreamed this up never had sex before *they* were married? Scary, real scary. Not that we shouldn't learn to say no and abstain, that's important, too. But, hey, how about stressing contraceptives and how not to pick up venereal diseases and how to avoid pregnancy? How about talking about drug use and dirty needles and not mingling blood and safe sex practices? How about talking straight about AIDS and how it's this virus that trashes the immune system and how it's one hundred percent fatal? How about getting real?

How can young people ever have a healthy, open attitude about their bodies when society treats sex as a four-letter word?

Hollywood—a place where people from Iowa mistake themselves for movie stars.

Fred Allen (1894–1956) comedian

HILDA

Gym is not her favorite period.

Twice a week I've got gym. Or gym's got me, I should say. Twice a week I have to get undressed and shove my good clothes in a cramped, mildewed, smelly locker and put on a this ratty looking outfit and get all steamed up and sweaty and then take a shower with a bunch of screaming, giggling girls who stare at my boobs. It's a humiliating, disgusting mess that doesn't prove squat.

My gym teacher is Miss Strickland. Or, Ms. Strickland, I mean. With a big, deep accent on the (*In a deep voice.*) *Ms.* The woman has muscles in her hair, I swear to you, and a real deep voice that sounds like it's coming from the bottom of a drain pipe. She was an athletic whiz in college and she thinks everybody's as strong as she is. The other day she had me trying to climb a rope to the top of the gym. What am I, a monkey here? Besides, what's it prove? How many times in her life does a woman need to shinny up twenty feet of hemp?

She also teaches Phys-ed. Another lame-o subject you leave in class the second you walk out the door. Stuff about the benefits of eating okra and how amino acids work and how the body functions. And she really gets off on it. When Strickland talks about the building blocks of nutrition she gets this wild far-out look in her eye like my father gets when he watches professional wrestling on TV—crazed.

Twice a week, I come home from school feeling awful and looking like hell, like I just cleaned out an attic, or rotated a set of tires, or something, you know. I'm a real mess! All because of gym. Because I have to tie myself in knots and jump up and down and strain and play stupid games and sweat like a pig and be humiliated by being naked and having to stuff my good clothes into a space the size of a shoe box.

I hate Gym. I can't stand it. It's stupid! It's life's biggest incentive for graduating from high school.

---

*I was born at the age of twelve on
the Metro-Goldwyn-Mayer lot.*

July Garland (Frances Gumm) (1922–1969)

CARRIE

Carrie expresses concern for the homeless.

Lots of times, when I'm on my way home from school in the afternoon, I see like these homeless people. More and more of them lately it seems, too. Used to be there were just a few of them here and there in doorways and on the sidewalks, and stuff. Now it seems like they're everywhere.

At first, these people really turned me off. So far as I was concerned, they were nothing but these dirty, worthless bums who should be working for a living instead of loafing. So, I refused to even look at them. I'd cross the street to avoid them. But when I did, you know, deep down inside, avoiding them always made me feel creepy. There was something deep inside that told me that it was shameful to ignore these people, to turn away.

Most homeless people have this real sad look on their faces, like somebody has turned them upside down and poured out all their happiness. There's nothing in their eyes—nothing. No brightness, no sparkle—just hopelessness, that's all. Here they are, men and women, out on the streets in all kinds of weather, begging for food, living like creatures instead of human beings. A real downer, you know.

Mr. Lansford, our sociology teacher, says a lot of homeless people are disenfranchised; that is, they're deprived because of unfortunate circumstances and have a good reasons for being on the streets. Like being laid-off work or losing everything overnight or having physical and mental problems, and like that. Once I understood more about them, once I knew where they were coming from, I didn't cross the street when I saw them anymore. Instead, I listened to what my insides were saying to me. They were saying: Carrie, like these are human beings, living, breathing people with feelings just like you and they deserve to be treated like you'd want to be.

I've got a feeling if people would listen when their insides talk the world would be a whole lot better place to live in.

A sex symbol is a thing. I hate being a thing.

Marilyn Monroe (Norma Jean Baker or Mortenson)
(1926–1962)

MARIA

Maria's boyfriend, Reggie, places her number one—after sports! Here she registers her complaint to him in no uncertain terms.

Like gimme a break here, okay? I mean, every night you're gonna have basketball practice? Maybe even Christmas Eve? Hey! What about me here? What about me walking home alone every night like some rejected nerd because you're in the gym? Do I count here? Do I exist? (*Pause for response.*) I know you can't get out of it, I know that, but at least you can come over after practice once in a while. (*Pause for response.*) Too tired? Whadaya mean, too tired? You're not too tired to copy my homework though, are you? Not too tired when it comes to ripping off my brain.

I used to think dating a basketball star was cool. Now I'm thinking maybe it sucks. Now I'm thinking about, maybe, David Johnson. (*Pause for response.*) So, he's in drama, so what? (*Pause for response.*) He is not! Just because a guy goes out for drama doesn't mean he's gay. That's just more of your macho basketball mentality, you turkey!

Yeah, and that's another thing. When we're together on weekends all you talk about is sports. (*Pause for response.*) So what? So, what about *me?* I don't count? Or do I come in a weak third after the Celtics and the Lakers? (*Pause for response.*) Yeah, sure sure, like I've heard that one before.

All I've got to say, Reggie, is that maybe you don't really care about me anymore, you know. Like maybe all you really care about is hanging out with a bunch of dorks whose shoe sizes are bigger than their IQs. Maybe you'd better find someone else you can steal homework from so you won't flunk out of basketball, because I've had it, okay? Like this whole thing just isn't happening anymore. You're too self-centered and inconsiderate.

And besides, you're way too tall.

When I saw my first screen test I ran from the projection room screaming.

Bette Davis (Ruth Elizabeth Davis) (1908–1989)

LAURIE

Laurie enjoys participation on the swim team but finds the training regimen grueling and restrictive to her social activities.

I like swimming a lot. I mean, like, it's neat being on the team and getting to travel to other schools and compete, and that. And when we win, we're all heros for a few days and the rest of the kids treat us like stars instead of a bunch of jocks for a while, and that's neat.

We practice every day for two hours and have to do special exercises and study techniques, and stuff. And we have to watch what we eat, too. We eat lots of carbs. We carb-load like crazy. Pasta, bread, grains of all kinds. Carbs give you energy, and when you specialize in the butterfly, like me, you need all the energy you can get. We also do weight training three times a week—with free weights.

As much as I like swimming, I'm starting to get burned out with it. I mean, the training, plus my regular school load, doesn't give me time for anything else. I mean, like gimme a break here, okay? But my parents are real hot on the swimming thing and they keep pushing me. Sometimes I don't know whether swimming means more to me or them. Lately, I think—them. Yeah, they really get off on my success. They have all of my trophies and medals and clippings and pictures right out on display in the living room. They had a bunch of shelves built to hold all the stuff. I'm beginning to feel like a show horse, or something, instead of a person.

I almost never date. I haven't got time. I'm either studying or swimming or weight lifting. And when I go on a date, I have to watch what I eat and be home early so I can get nine hours sleep like the coach wants. And all of the weight training is starting to build me up too much. I'm getting way too big for a girl. Hey, I want to look feminine, not like some overdeveloped muscle-head. I want to be able to fit into hot clothes instead of sweats and over-sized T-shirts. Guys are turned-off by muscle-bound women. What guy wants to go out with a girl who can bench press more than he can?

I'm about to give mom and dad the word. I mean, I know they're real proud of me and everything, but, like, I'm getting real fed up with spending thirty-percent of my life under water.

The play's the thing
Wherein I'll catch the conscience of the King.

William Shakespeare. *Hamlet*, II:2

TINA

Tina is greatly bereaved by the passing of her English teacher.

I had this chip on my shoulder about English. Most of school, for that matter. So far as I was concerned, the whole scene was a big waste of time. Until I got into Mrs. Montez's class, that is. She had this kind, easy way about her. And she didn't pressure you. She had this way of teaching that made things interesting and made you curious. Like about poetry. I always hated poetry. I mean, like what good is it? But then, one day, she read us this poem called "After Midnight" by Louis Simpson:

The dark streets are deserted
With only a drugstore glowing
Softly, like a sleeping body;

With one white, naked bulb
In the back, that shines
On suicides and abortions.

Who lives in these dark houses?
I am suddenly aware
I might live here myself.

The garage man returns
And puts the change in my hand,
Counting the singles carefully.*

When she read about the drugstore glowing like a sleeping body it really knocked me out. Wow! "Softly, like a sleeping body." I could just see it like that; see the drugstore glowing there dead-like on this dark, lonely street. (*Pause.*)

Mrs. Montez died last week. Of cancer. I guess she'd had it for a long time. We all knew she was sick because she said she was and she used to be off work a lot. But we never knew that is was . . . I mean, we didn't know she was going to die. I really miss her. A lot. She was a special person who cared. And she turned me around. Now I read everything I can. And I love poetry. It's my favorite because it lets you see things from like different angles. I think poetry's the best. I'm even writing some myself. This is what I wrote about Mrs. Montez:

Her voice was tender
And made you want to learn
More and more

Because when she spoke
She spoke only to you
And made you feel alive.

---

*"After Midnight" by Louis Simpson, from *Selected Poems*, Harcourt Brace Jovanovich, Inc.

RACHEL

Rachel has overcome her stage fright and is now an enthusiastic participant in dramatics.

My friend, Barbara Wells, she's like this big deal in drama. Like, she does most of the leads in the school plays and has already done two commercials.

Barb has always been real interested in acting ever since she was a little kid. She used to dress up in weird outfits and put on plays in her garage for the kids in the neighborhood. I was in a couple of them and it always made me nervous and self-conscious and I used to get tongue-tied and couldn't remember my lines. But it was easy for Barbara. She never got nervous. Being in front of a bunch of people never seemed to bother her at all.

She'd been after me to join dramatics for a long time. But I was too afraid to get into it, like too shy. Then one day she calls me up and says that one of the girls in her class had to transfer and that they were right in the middle of getting this scene ready and they were desperate and, like, I was perfect for this part and she begged me to take it. It was the part of one of the three sisters in this play by Chekhov. He writes these plays where people stand around all dressed up like store dummies and rap for hours about nothing. But anyway, Barb was on the spot and really in a bad place so I said okay.

At first, I was really nervous. But once I got into it, I was okay. Even though my character did have some pretty stupid lines. Stuff like: (*Overly dramatic with her hand to her head.*) "It's you who are stupid, Olya. I love him, that's my destiny, that's my fate. And he loves me. It's frightening, isn't it?" Off-the-wall garbage like that. The pits. But we did the scene and people said I was great and that made me feel good and now I'm in drama full time. And I really enjoy it. Although a lot of the stuff we do is pretty lame or very old-timey or awfully juvenile. Our drama teacher says it's hard to find good material for young people.

I think maybe we should do more stuff by writers like Chekhov. The more I think about it—he's not so bad.

When you got the personality,
you don't need the nudity.

Mae West (1892–1980)

DARLENE

She recalls the tragedy of senseless violence.

We were all standing around outside school talking like always. Nobody had any reason to suspect anything bad was going to happen.

I was talking to Letta Jackson and Mary Chin when there were like these popping noises. Pop, pop, pop! Like that. At first we didn't think anything of it because they were just like these little cracking noises like when firecrackers go off, you know. Then I saw Shirley Whitmer fall to the ground. Then Jason Goldman goes down, too. Then there were more popping sounds and some other kids fell and then we knew what was happening and everybody screamed and ran in all directions. It was terrible.

Near some hedges I saw this guy drop this gun and run off like crazy down Franklin Street. He jumped into a car and tore off. All around me kids were crying and hysterical and screaming and teachers were shouting. Everybody was going crazy. It was really hell!

I could see a pool of blood spreading out around Mary Jackson's head and she wasn't moving and I knew she just had to be dead. Shirley Whitmer, too. She was dead, too. You could tell by the way she was lying there with her legs twisted under her. I'd never seen a dead person before, but I knew she was.

There was—there was like this extra special stillness to her that let me know.

The sniper killed four kids and wounded three. Two are going to be okay. The other, Janet Clark, is paralyzed for life. A bunch of us went over to the hospital to visit her the other day. We took her flowers and some books. She talked to us and smiled and was very brave.

I don't hang around outside school, anymore. Most of the kids don't. Because you have these memories and fears. I don't think school will ever be the same. Maybe not my life, even. When you see something like this it does something to you inside, it changes you. I used to think that all people were okay and the world was safe. Now I know different.

I don't want to be thought of as wholesome.
Julie Andrews (Julia Wells) (1934–)

VICKY

Vicky resents the imposition of rules regarding her after-school activities.

Twice a week, after school, we have these dumb dances in the gym where everyone stands around listening to square sounds that are piped in over the PA system; where everybody checks out everybody else and knows what everybody is thinking. Which is something really crappy about the way you look and dress and dance, and stuff. Kids really get-off on trashing each other. I guess that's half the fun of being young.

After school we used to hang out at this place called The Pit over on third street where they had bitchin' bands who were really into what was happening musically. The Raunch Brothers were my favorite because they were into heavy-duty sounds and rap and they dressed bizarre with chains and ripped jeans, and black gloves with spikes on 'em. One dude had this really cool hair that was bright orange with purple streaks. Wow, was he ever cute. His name was Mondo.

But our the parents freaked because we were hanging out at The Pit. So, they got together and made it tough on the place so they had to close in the afternoons. Then they came up with this insane idea of having dances in the gym where everybody hates to be because it's still school and the place smells like a jock strap and the sound system is the worst and the music bounces around because the place is like this big, ugly, stinking cavern. And the music? Hey, like do me a favor! The Beatles,

Jan and Dean, Bobby Vinton, and a lot of other stupid, sixties junk. Bobby Vinton? Soon as I graduate, I'm outta here for college. Some place a zillion miles from home where nobody will be able to tell me what kind of music to listen to; where I'll be able to hang out where they're playing decent sounds. Someplace like The Pit. Someplace with class.

All this time I've just wanted to be blonde, beautiful, and 5 feet 2 inches tall.

Beatrice Arthur (Beatrice Frankel) (1923–)

LISA

Lisa finds contradictions between what she is taught and the realities of the political process.

I still have problems when it comes to politics. Even though Mr. Willis explains a lot about how the political system works.

It seems like politics in real life is a whole lot different from what we learn in school. We learn about how, as a politician, you're supposed to work for the good of the people who elect you. I mean, like it's your responsibility to serve, you know. That's the basic thing I get out of it, anyway. After all of the complicated stuff Mr. Willis teaches us about democracy and legislation, the electoral process, and the rest of it, the bottom line is—to serve.

But it seems to me that politicians are more concerned with bickering than serving; with spending money where it will help them get re-elected instead of putting it where it's really needed.

Recently the State legislature voted against more money for teachers' salaries. They said they were already being paid enough and that the State's budget wouldn't allow more. Then they turn right around and give themselves this big pay raise. Not that they don't deserve it, maybe they do. But how about the teachers? Hey, what about them? Teachers are extremely important and they should be paid like they are.

Teachers deserve just as much salary as accountants, aerospace people, and others in the private sector any day of the week. Maybe even more considering their importance to the future of our society. After all, without proper schooling what chance do you have?

When you stop to analyze it, where would all the doctors, lawyers, people in aerospace, and other professionals be if they hadn't gotten a proper education? I get that underpaying our teachers is being very short-sighted.

I also get the impression that politics is a crock.

I used to tremble from nerves so badly that the only way I could hold my head steady was to lower my chin practically to my chest and look up at Bogie. That was the beginning of The Look.

Lauren Bacall (Betty Jean Perske) (1924–)

MEGAN

Megan, a rape victim, finds returning to school difficult.

It's really hard coming back to school now. I mean, it's so embarrassing, you know. It's awful having people look at you like you're some kind of freak, or something.

My whole life has changed. I mean, nothing's the same. I feel different now and I'm kind of still in shock. And I don't feel young anymore. It's like all-of-a-sudden I got old.

It's been more than a month now since I was, was. . . . Since it happened. But it seems like only yesterday because the thing's on my mind constantly and I can't seem to get it out. I don't think I'll ever be able to. Mom says in time I'll get over it. Maybe. I don't know. I just keep reliving the whole thing and it's, like, this nightmare but worse because you know it actually happened.

After the police arrested him I had to go down and identify him and it was awful because I felt ashamed. Even though I was the victim, I felt cheap and ugly and guilty. The guy was there with his lawyer and he was real arrogant and he kept glaring at me the whole time like I was so much dirt.

It happened when I was cutting though Snyder Park. He pulled up in his car and rolled down his window and asked me directions. When I got close, he threw open the door and grabbed me and. . . . (*She nearly breaks down.*)

(*Regaining her composure.*) Afterwards, I walked around in this daze crying and feeling angry. At first, I wasn't going to tell anyone. It was almost two days before I told my mom because I was so ashamed.

And I still feel ashamed. Even though I have nothing to be ashamed of. And people treat me differently now, too. My boyfriend, Russ Harper, I never see him anymore. He won't have anything to do with me.

Instead of treating me like a slut, you'd think people would be understanding and kind. Some are. A few. But a lot have this attitude like it was my fault. My fault! Can you believe it!

You know, I think what hurts almost as much as being raped is realizing how cruel and petty and narrow-minded people can be. And it's changed me. Like I said . . . all-of-a-sudden, I feel old.

YOUNG MEN

RUDY

Rudy, now clean, recalls his days of drug and alcohol dependency.

I used to be like this regular, normal kid who was on the track team and who played baseball and liked school, you know. I mean, like, I was a good student who never got into trouble, or anything, and I got along good with everybody. Then I started hanging out with these kids after school who were into drinking and doing dope. I thought they were neat because they were so much different than me, I guess. I mean, like, they always seemed so cool. It was like they were grown up and above all of the high school stuff, you know.

I started out with beer and a few hits maybe two, three afternoons a week. Then I'd jump on three or four beers and destroy a joint. Then I just kept going from there. It's like you're on this ride at an amusement park and the faster you go the better it feels so you wanna keep on stepping up the tempo, you know.

Next I got into these things called mushrooms. Mushrooms had, like, this reverse effect. The best way I can describe mushrooms is, like, they use up all of your happy cells. They make you feel real down and out of it. But by then I was in too deep to fall back. So, I went on to free-base and then to heroin which made me throw up and tremble. I was really hooked and strung-out.

My habits were costing me around eighty bucks a day so I had to steal to support them. I was in big trouble and I was off-the-wall most of the time and hostile and I looked bad and was dressing like a bum.

I was lucky the police caught me when they did, because I was on the way out, man. And I was lucky my parents were cool and that I was able to get help from people who cared. Now I'm clean and I intend to stay that way.

The thing is—don't start up on anything. 'Cause that way you can't move on up to something heavier. And don't kid yourself—anyone can get hooked, anyone. Like me. Here I was this normal kid who almost totalled his life.

I'm old, I'm young, I'm intelligent,
I'm stupid. My tide goes in and out.

Warren Beatty (Warren Beaty) (1937–)

DANNY

Danny shows concern for the state of the environment..

Old Man Nichols is this brainy dude who teaches us science, okay? And even though he dresses like he does his shopping at Wal-Mart, he's a real ace when it comes to science. He knows what's happening.

For the past couple of days he's been into, like, what's happening with the ozone layer, you know. It's like this protective layer above the earth that filters out the sun's rays so's they don't go ape and burn the living hell outta everything and everybody; so we don't all, like, become extra-crispy fried chicken overnight. The ozone layer is neat. A lot of things about the planet are neat.

Old man Nichols says that, like, we're losing the ozone layer because of people burning all of these fossil fuels and stuff like crazy and because of the international over-use of hydrofluorocarbons—the stuff that's in the compressors of refrigerators and in spray cans, and like that. He says that this junk is really trashing our environment and that they've already found a couple a holes in the ozone layer and, like, it's getting real dangerous because if we don't stop goofing up the sun's gonna radiate the hell outta us and cause cancers, and everything.

When you stop to think about it, this here is very scary stuff, Waldo. Do you realize we could become baked potatoes while crusing in your convertible? Or how about going for a tan and coming up looking like bacon rinds? Like, think about it, man.

People had better start shaping up fast and thinking about the planet and stop laying trash on everything before we all turn back into giant lizards. I'm gonna do my part, I know that for sure. You're damned right, I am! I'm not dating any more sluts who use hair spray.

I was in show business straight from the womb.
Robby Benson (Robert Segal) (1956–)

ROD

Rod recalls a stabbing incident.

This guy, Eddie Greene, he was always kind of strange. He always hung to himself and was never very friendly. I tried to talk to him a couple of times but he was never in touch; he always seemed way off somewhere like on another planet, or something. A weird dude. And lately he was getting weirder. For one thing, he started carrying a knife and he got his jollies out of showing it to everyone. And he started talking real loud and boisterous and he was using a lot of profanity. Like I said, he was getting very weird.

Then, a couple of weeks ago, in fifth-period English, Eddie gets into this argument with another guy and he's screaming bad language and being obnoxious and the teacher, Mrs. Alvarez, had to come down on him hard before he'd cool it. But then, afterwards, he kept disrupting the class with all these off-the-wall rowdy comments to the point where nobody could do any work. So, Mrs. Alvarez said she was going to write him up and that she wanted to have a meeting with his parents. So, she started writing out a referral slip. Okay?

Then, all-of-a-sudden, Eddie gets up and goes to the to front of the room and sticks his knife in Mrs. Alvarez's back, just like that. I couldn't believe it, man. Just like that, the crazy bastard stabs her! A bunch of us guys jumped on him and held him till security got there.

Mrs. Alvarez was in the hospital for a week. She's at home now recovering. She still can't believe what happened, can't understand it. She doesn't know if she'll come back or not. And who the hell could blame her if she didn't?After something like that? I know I wouldn't. They couldn't pay me enough to get me to work in a jungle. No way, man. Forget it.

What's happening to this world anymore, anyway? It's even getting too dangerous to teach.

An actor's a guy who, if you ain't talking about him, ain't listening.

Marlon Brando (1924–)

DON

Don finds great difficulty in verbalizing his feelings.

It's not like I can't get to talk to my teachers, because I can. It's
. . . it's just that I don't, that's all. I just can't bring myself to.
It's . . . it's too hard for me to say stuff. It's the same way at
home, too. I can't seem to open up and say what's really going
on deep down inside me. Because if I'd tell people what I
really think, about the stuff that's really super-important to me,
they'd never understand. No way. And besides, I get the feeling
they really don't give a damn anyway.

It's like I don't feel good about myself. I feel like I'm like
second rate, or worse; like I'm not good enough to have
friends, or for people to like me. And I feel conspicuous and
out of place most of the time, too. Like everybody's looking at
me because I'm this . . . this nothing.

Hey, I mean . . . who do you tell stuff like this to? Your
folks, your teachers—other kids? Forget it. I was gonna talk to
Mr. Hathaway after school the other day but when I went to his
office he was on the phone and he kept looking at me like I was
a nobody. At least that's the way I felt; like he didn't want to
listen to a bunch of stuff from a zero person like me. Besides, if
I ever told Hathaway how I really felt—real down and
depressed all the time and lonely and real mad at people
because I don't think they like me—if I ever told him that, he'd
think I was crazy.

I don't know what to do. I really don't. It's kinda like I'm stuck on dead-center, you know. I know I need to talk to somebody, but I don't know who or how. My life's, like, at this standstill right now and I can't seem to break free and get it moving.

I don't know what the hell to do. I want people to understand me, you know, to like me, I really do. But it's real hard to get people to understand and like you when you don't understand and like yourself.

My acting technique is to look up at God just
before the camera rolls and say, 'Give me a break.'
James Caan (1938–)

RICK

Rick scoffs at the suggestion he has a chance with Sherry Hill.

Are you kidding? Sherry Hill is a fox. And built. Whoa! This
lady wasn't born like normal people, she was manufactured.
Nobody gets a body like that from normal childbirth—nobody.
She's ace-number-one. And you think I should ask her for a
date. Me, ask *her* out? Me? Gimme a break here, man. Sherry
Hill doesn't date peons. She goes out with guys with bucks.
Like Larry Shirtzer. His old man owns Shirtzer Realty. They
live over on the North side in a house that looks like a hotel, or
a castle, or something. You've seen his wheels, haven't you? A
brand-new BMW. And how about his clothes? Like the latest,
Italian designer stuff that costs a fortune. One of his suits is
worth more than my car. How do you expect a guy like me to
compete with someone like this, anyway? A guy with a rusted-
out, ten-year-old Plymouth with bald tires, seven faded T-
shirts, two pairs of jeans, a hand-me-down sports jacket, and a
pair of blown-out Nikes? No chance, man.

Besides, she doesn't know I'm on the planet. She sits across
the isle from me in English and when she looks at me it's like
she's looking through a window. I'm not even there, ya know?
It's like I'm the Invisible Man. And you expect me to hit on a
woman like this? Do me a favor, Charlie. I've got enough
problems without total rejection here, okay? Without getting
the big freeze.

I'll just stay loose and cool and live on my own plateau and date down-to-earth ladies within my financial range of burgers and fries. Sherry Hill and I are like oil and water, from two different worlds. Get real, man. (*Pause.*) She did? She said that? Naw, c'mon. Bullshit. (*Pause.*) She did? She thinks I'm cute? She thinks I'm cool? Naw. You're putting me on, man. (*Pause.*) Really? She actually did. For real? No kidding? (*Pause.*) I'll be damned.

Hey! All right! Wow. Hey, like maybe I'll give her a call. But not right away.

Let the bitch eat her heart out.

I have always hated that
James Bond. I'd like to kill him.

Sean Connery (Thomas Connery) (1929–)

ROBERT

From Robert's speech we get the idea that cafeteria food isn't exactly gourmet.

It's the worst, man, the worst, below the bottom of the pit. I only eat in the cafeteria when I'm short on money or haven't got time to go out. The stuff they dish up down there is like hospital food, or something, you know. Everything they make tastes exactly the same and is real soft and mushy like for old people without teeth. Like Jello, for instance. They always have Jello every day in about ninety barfy flavors ranging from cherry to knotty pine. Topped off with some kind of whipped cream that looks like dirty cement.

And then they have these dishes with names where you can't figure out what's really in them. Like Turkey Surprise. Hey! Like I know what turkey is, but what's the "surprise," man? Tell me about the "surprise." But they never do. Seems like nobody down there ever knows what the "surprise" is. That's because they're afraid to tell you it's wet sawdust.

There's always stuff like this on the menu every day. Mystery stuff that you gotta be super brave to try. Stuff like Fiesta Rice and Country Chowder and Shepherd's Pie. What the hell's in Shepherd's Pie, anyway? The last time I tried it, I think, maybe, an old shepherd's socks.

They come up with some real far-out, pukey concoctions, all right. Stuff like Vegetable Medley, Spanish Bean Soup, and Sweet and Sour Turkey over Rice. Ooooh! Real appetizing, huh? Like their tuna sandwiches that are so runny the tuna pours out of the bread and runs all over your hands and you smell like fish for hours. I call it blender tuna. Then, sometimes, every now and then, they go all out and have pizza. But like it's like this pizza from hell. Kind of like toasted white bread loaded with catsup. The last time I ate it I threw up in my gym bag.

The cafeteria's like the restaurant of last resort, ya know. The only thing you can be really safe about down there is the water. And even that smells a lot like Turkey Surprise. And the school's always hyping nutrition, too. Is this a crack-up, or what? Hey, you're better off at McDonald's anytime. The worst you get there is a bunch of over-salted grease.

*There is a mixture of anarchy
and discipline in the way I work.*

Robert De Niro (1943–)

ERNIE

Ernie has moved from a major metropolitan area in order to escape the gangs, save himself, live a life of social responsibility. Here he speaks of the fears and pitfalls of a gang-related existence.

I feel like I'm a free person since me and my folks moved here and I started in going to this school. I feel free for the first time since I was twelve when I started kicking with gang guys.

You kind of ease into a gang, ya know? My buddy was a gang-banger—in and out of jail—so, I just kind of followed along. My mother would say, "No, get out." But it didn't do no good, man. I didn't listen. I'd hang out and come home stoned. I din't think about nothing. I just got high and did whatever came up, man, just did it. Who cares, ya know.

We were, like, a club at first. We only met to party, but then some guys from another gang brought guns in and people got shot. They shot one of our home-boys and we shot them. It made no sense, ya know, what were we doing? The scariest place is your own neighborhood. All I ever thought about was being killed.

The last time I got busted for robbery, they sent me to this juvenile probation camp out in the sticks, ya know. It was my second time. While I was there I got to thinking that I had to get out of the gangs, ya know, leave the city. But you've got to get far away, man, or they'll find you. A friend will find you, or an enemy. You just don't step in and out of a gang, man. You step in and they lock the door behind you.

But I knew I had to get out, get far away, because while I was at the camp I kept dreaming about dying. I, like, kept seeing myself being shot and then I felt myself, ya know, fading away, and I'd wake up sweating, man, really shaking. I can't tell you the feeling.

I used to hear guys say like they'd die for their neighborhoods; but, ya know, man, when you think about it . . . dying is a scary thing.

Acting is a question of absorbing other people's personalities and some of your own experience.

Paul Newman (1925–)

RALPH

The plight of the homeless is of great concern .

Like, I see 'em on the way to and from school everyday. They hang out on the streets and in doorways and a lot of 'em have, like, these little lean-to homes over in the park. I never used to give 'em much thought. They were just like these bums hanging-out and hitting on everybody for change. Until last week.

As I was walking home from school, this real tattered looking guy goes and collapses right in front of me. Just goes and tumbles over. Just like that. It really shook me up. I'd never seen anyone pass out before. I didn't know what was happening; if he was stoned or drunk or sick or dead, or what. I didn't know what to do. And he was really cruddy. You don't want to touch people like that, you know. But I just had to do something. I mean, after all. . . .

So, I went over and grabbed him under the arms and got him to a bus bench and sat him down and he thanked me. He was real dirty and had this straggly beard but he had bright, intelligent eyes that were kind and knowing.

I started talking to him and it turns out he used to be a successful printer who had a family and kids, and everything. Then his wife left him and his business went bad and he fell apart mentally and took to the streets.

I took him over to the Donut Shop and bought him some donuts and coffee and he perked up. He hadn't eaten in almost two days. That's the reason he'd crashed. Because he was so weak. His name is Mike and he's a neat guy and I'm going to help him all I can. My dad says maybe he can help out around his store.

I used to think all street people were scum-bags, that all they were into was dodging work and bumming spare change for booze money. But now I know this isn't always the case. A lot of them are poor down-and-out individuals whose lives have fallen apart and who are looking for something more than a handout. They're looking for help and understanding.

I heard this expression one time that makes a lot of sense to me now. That you really don't know about people till you walk a mile in their shoes.

---

*Whatever success I've had is due
to a lot of instinct and a little luck.*

Clint Eastwood (1930–)

DARRYL

Darryl reveals his misconceptions regarding dramatics.

If someone had told me I'd be in a play this year, I would have said they were out of it. The last thing I ever wanted to do was get up in front of a bunch of people and act. Like track was my thing, you know—low hurdles. And besides, I always figured all the guys in dramatics for being sort of strange. Like guys whose favorite color is magenta, know what I mean. The whole bunch of dramatic freaks, the girls *and* the guys, they always seemed to be like these off-the-wall lame-os who couldn't find it with both hands.

Like Rodney Marchbanks, this super-strange dude who came out for track the first day with this play *Hamlet*. He sat around reading and screaming Shakespeare while the rest of us guys were busting our buns. Coach Roberts got ticked and made him do laps. But Marchbanks didn't bitch. He just went ahead and did laps while still reading this *Hamlet* garbage.

Next day, the coach teams Marchbanks up with me and Corky Johnson and Elwood Clark and Dick Lawrence on the low hurdles and the dude stands there real cool before the heat reading over his stupid *Hamlet*. He didn't even warm up, this guy. When it's time to race, he stuffs the play into the back of his shorts and gets set. When Coach Roberts drops his hand Marchbanks disappears—vanishes! Zoom! Like I've never seen a guy run that fast, ever. It was like he was this bullet shot out of a gun, you know.

Rodney and I became friends. He's a good dude. And, *Hamlet?* Hey, it isn't all that bad either, not really. Even though the main stud acts like a spaz half the time and sees ghosts and wants to knock off every other person he knows.

When Marchbanks said I shoult try out for the part of Polonius, this old guy in *Hamlet* who's real shifty and weird, I told him to forget it. Me, in *Hamlet?* But he kept insisting. So, I finally went by dramatics and read for the part and, guess what—I got it. Mrs. Fox, the dramatics teacher, said that I was, like, this natural talent.

So, now I'm in dramatics. I dropped out of track because it got in the way of play rehearsals. Besides, dramatics beats the living crap out of low hurdles. And everyday I get to do these scenes with great looking ladies and I don't have to worry about busting up my knees.

Tragedy is if I cut my finger. Comedy is if I walk into an open sewer and die.

Mel Brooks (Melvin Kaminsky) (1926–)

BEN

Ben speaks passionately regarding the "gift of life."

Last year in school we had this discussion about the "gift of life." You know, donating your organs so they can be used to benefit the living. Well, afterwards, my twin brother, Michael, and I thought it sounded like a good idea so we talked over donating our organs with our parents and they thought it was a good idea, too. In fact, because of our discussion, our whole family—my mom and dad and my sister—we all signed the necessary papers and donated our organs.

You all know about my brother Mike being fatally injured during football practice. Well, he never regained consciousness and was pronounced brain-dead and was in intensive care for weeks before he died. It was a terrible thing. This is the first time I've been able to talk about it. (*Beat.*) The one thing that helped us all a lot was that we knew that Mike wouldn't be totally dead; that some of him would be living on in other people and saving lives. This was a real satisfaction. (*He pulls a letter from his pocket.*) Let me read you part of a letter we received from the University of Alabama.

"Dear Mr. and Mrs. Rinker and Family: On behalf of the Alabama Organ and Tissue Center, may I express my deepest sympathy to you and your family for the tragic loss of your son, Mike. I would also like to express my gratitude. I admire your ability to express your love for Mike by allowing his death to give the 'gift of life' to others.

"Both of Mike's kidneys were transplanted at our hospital. One was received by a twenty-three year old female, the other by a forty-eight year old male. Both recipients experienced immediate function, and are returning to their families to live normal lives free of dialysis.

"We located a woman suffering from coronary artery disease in need of a transplant. She is the mother of six children. She is in intensive care recovering without complications. The bone will be stored here at the University Hospital to be used at Children's Hospital and throughout Alabama in the treatment of spinal deformities in children and in patients suffering from orthopedic injuries and disease. These patients look forward to lives without crutches, braces, or wheelchairs.

"The eye foundation will soon inform you about how the corneas were used. Can you imagine what it must be like for these patients who have lived in darkness to regain this most precious gift of sight?" (*He folds the letter and returns it to his pocket.*)

There's more, but that's the idea of it. Maybe some of you guys will want to give the "gift of life," too. It's a good thing to do.

TONY

Here Tony relates his McDonald's work experience.

I mean, like, I've got nothing against working. Working's cool, okay? It's a good thing if you wanna generate bucks. But, like, some jobs make you feel like a stupid slob instead of a legitimate working person. Like, let me give you a for instance: I see this gigantic sign in McDonald's window advertising for help, okay? Like advertising for regular help plus, get this— "Managerial Positions Open." Big deal. Like, if you're lucky, you get to be a manager after five years of dishing up grease. But anyway, I figured like this was a good, quick way to make some extra dough so I'd be able to take out Sue Ann Walters to half-way decent place every now and then. So, I fill out this application that's as long as your car, and they hire me.

Now, the first day they give me this lame outfit to wear, okay? Like this clown outfit the color of baby poop and this little cap that's makes you look like a monkey. When I ask the manager if I can wear my own stuff, my jeans and that, he say's that that isn't the McDonald's image.

The manager was about five feet tall and weighed in at about two-fifty. He was this living testimonial to a lifetime diet of Big Macs. A walking mountain of fat. Wow! And he's like this career McDonald's person who runs the place like it's an army camp and struts around wearing a headset screaming orders to people who he refers to as "ladies" and "gentlemen."

I figure I'm going to be tossing together burgers and junk, right? No way. Because I'm the new guy they make me do all the crummy stuff. Like cleaning up the restrooms and mopping up the floor every twenty minutes with this strong smelling detergent that'll take the skin off an elephant.

So, like here I am this restroom attendant mop-up person in a dumb outfit the color of crap and guess who walks in? Sue Ann Walters. Fact is, I didn't see her at first and I almost trashed her shoes with this liquid acid I'm wiping up the floor with. It was, like, real embarrassing, you know. I wanted to freak, but I kept my cool and tipped my monkey cap to her like some big awkward dork.

And then, guess what? Then she goes and slips and falls flat on her butt because I forgot to put up the "Caution Wet Floor" sign, okay? Then Mr. Lardo, the manager, he waddles over and starts giving me lip right there in front of everybody. Creep. That did it. I threw my cap into the mop bucket and walked out. I mailed back the rest of their stupid outfit in a trash bag.

Sue Ann Walters hasn't returned my calls in over two weeks. A guy has to be real careful where he takes a job.

RICHARD

He questions the archaic attitudes regarding teen sex.

I don't know if it's my teachers or my parents, or what. But when it comes to talking straight about sex, forget it. They hedge and beat around the bush and act embarrassed like sex doesn't exist between high school kids. Are they really this naive? Or are they just plain out of it?

It's totally amazing how adults become more childish than children when the subject of sex is brought up. It's like, whoa! get outta here with that stuff. They still persist in treating something very real like it's this big, ugly, dirty secret. Here we are putting guys on the moon and traveling faster than sound but when it comes to the naked human body doing normal functions the earth is still flat, you know.

No wonder we have teen pregnancy and disease. And even some cases of AIDS. And why shouldn't we? For the most part sex is still underground, something you find out about for yourself in the back seat of a car. Why can't our teachers and parents and government face up to the fact that young people make it? They always have and always will. Just like all of them did, too, probably, if they were human, that is. Sex is like part of us. Like eating and sleeping. But with eating and sleeping they tell you all about nutrition and where you can go to buy an extra-firm mattress. But, hey, no such luck when it comes to sex. They run from the subject like it's a pit bull, or

something, avoid discussing it. Like that nasty word—
"condom." Whoa! You say that, they jump twenty-feet. Or how
about that "real scary" street expression—"rubber?" Wow!
Look out Sam! Wash your mouth out with soap, and then go
stand in the corner.

Hey! How about the cold facts, the truth, the unvarnished
realities? How about facing the issues? How about recognizing
them and dealing with them straight-ahead without fear and
embarrassment?

---

*I didn't say actors are cattle. What I said
was, actors should be* treated *like cattle.*

Alfred Hitchcock (1899–1980)

COLIN

He stresses the critical role of the educator.

Last year we had a teacher's strike. It lasted almost twenty days. And it held up our grades and disrupted our studies and our regular routine of going to school. But, you know, I can't say that I blame the teachers for striking. Not after I read what their salaries were. Like, a lot of them were only making twenty-five thousand a year. Hey! Larry Montez made almost that much last year working part time and during summer vacation selling sporting goods at Meeks.

Quality education is super-important and it should be recognized and rewarded. Teachers should be treated fairly and be looked up to and respected because they're the ones with the responsibility of shaping tomorrow's citizens. We look up to the wrong people a lot, I think. Like, to the ones who make the most money. This seems to be the way we judge how important people are; by how much money they make and what they have. So far as I'm concerned, any of my teachers is a far more important person than some rock star or some guy who just signed a zillion dollar deal with the NBA. Teaching people how to think intelligently and preparing them for a solid future should be much more important than a hit CD or a slam dunk. But it isn't. 'Cause our value system is screwed.

ORDER DIRECT

MONOLOGUES THEY HAVEN'T HEARD, Karshner. Modern speeches written in the language of today. $7.95.

MORE MONOLOGUES THEY HAVEN'T HEARD, Karshner. More exciting living-language speeches. $7.95.

SCENES THEY HAVEN'T SEEN, Karshner. Modern scenes for men and women. $7.95.

FOR WOMEN, MONOLOGUES THEY HAVEN'T HEARD, Pomerance. Contemporary speeches for actresses. $7.95

MONOLOGUES FOR KIDS, Roddy. 28 wonderful speeches for boys and girls. $7.95.

MORE MONOLOGUES for KIDS, Roddy. More great speeches for boys and girls. $7.95.

SCENES FOR KIDS, Roddy. 30 scenes for girls and boys. $7.95.

MONOLOGUES FOR TEENAGERS, Karshner. Contemporary teen speeches. $7.95.

SCENES FOR TEENAGERS, Karshner. Scenes for today's teen boys and girls. $7.95.

HIGH SCHOOL MONOLOGUES THEY HAVEN'T HEARD, Karshner. Contemporary speeches for high schoolers, $7.95.

DOWN-HOME, Karshner. Speeches for men and women in the language of rural America. $7.95.

MONOLOGUES FROM THE CLASSICS, ed. Karshner. Speeches from Shakespeare, Marlowe and others. An excellent collection for men and women, $7.95.

SCENES FROM THE CLASSICS, ed. Maag. Scenes from Shakespeare and others. $7.95.

SHAKESPEARE'S MONOLOGUES THEY HAVEN'T HEARD, ed. Dotterer. Lesser known speeches from The Bard. $7.95.

MONOLOGUES FROM CHEKHOV, trans. Cartwright. Modern translations from Chekhov's major plays: *Cherry Orchard, Uncle Vanya, Three Sisters, The Sea Gull*. $7.95.

MONOLOGUES FROM GEORGE BERNARD SHAW, ed. Michaels. Great speeches for men and women from the works of G.B.S. $7.95.

MONOLOGUES FROM OSCAR WILDE, ed. Michaels. The best of Wilde's urbane, dramatic writing from his greatest plays. For men and women. $7.95.

WOMAN, Susan Pomerance. Monologues for actresses. $7.95.

WORKING CLASS MONOLOGUES, Karshner. Speeches from blue collar occupations. Waitress, cleaning lady, policewoman, truck driver, miner, etc. $7.95.

MODERN SCENES FOR WOMEN, Pomerance. Scenes for today's actresses. $7.95.

MONOLOGUES FROM MOLIERE, trans. Dotterer. A definitive collection of speeches from the French Master. The first translation into English prose. $7.95.

SHAKESPEARE'S MONOLOGUES FOR WOMEN, trans. Dotterer. $7.95.

DIALECT MONOLOGUES, Karshner/Stern. 13 essential dialects applied to contemporary monologues. Book and Cassette Tape. $19.95.

YOU SAID A MOUTHFUL, Karshner. Tongue twisters galore. Great exercises for actors, singers, public speakers. Fun for everyone. $7.95.

TEENAGE MOUTH, Karshner. Modern monologues for young men and women. $7.95.

SHAKESPEARE'S LADIES, Dotterer. A second book of Shakespeare's monologues for women. With a descriptive text on acting Shakespeare. $7.95.

BETH HENLEY:MONOLOGUES FOR WOMEN, Henley.*Crimes of the Heart* and others. $7.95.

CITY WOMEN, Smith. 20 powerful, urban monologues. Great audition pieces. $7.95.

KIDS' STUFF, Roddy. 30 great audition pieces for children. $7.95.

KNAVES, KNIGHTS, and KINGS, Dotterer. Speeches for men from Shakespeare. $8.95.

DIALECT MONOLOUES, VOL II, Karshner/Stern. 14 more important dialects. Farsi, Afrikaans, Asian Indian, etc. Book and Cassette tape. $19.95.

RED LICORICE, Tippit. 31 great scene-monologues for preteens. $7.95.

MODERN MONOLOGUES for MODERN KIDS, Mauro. $7.95.

SPEECHES & SCENES from OSCAR'S BEST FILMS. Dotterer. $19.95.

Your check or money order (no cash or COD) plus handling charges of $4.00 for the first book, and $1.50 for each additional book. California residents add 8.25 % tax. Send your order to: Dramaline Publications, 36-851 Palm View Road, Rancho Mirage, California 92270.